TABLE OF CONTENTS

Published 2020

NEW HAVEN PUBLISHING LTD

www.newhavenpublishingltd.com

newhavenpublishing@gmail.com

newhaven
publishing

ISBN: 978-1-912587-38-4

INTRODUCTION

At the beginning of 2020 we were about to celebrate our 500th episode of our celebrity talk show *Profiles*. In many ways it was also a time for reflection, after all, we've been on the air for twenty years interviewing one celebrity after another.

The memories and highlights run deep. Each interview has left a special lasting impression on everyone involved with the TV Series. Sometimes it's something that happened before or after the interview, other times it was something within the interview that remains with you. Nevertheless, after 500 episodes, I also realized that this program has been a huge part of our lives for over two decades.

Profiles has been airing on the NYC Media Network since 2003. We produce the series from our studios in Times Square in the heart of New York City. The series has a viewing demographic of 20 million potential viewers in a 50 million radius of New York City, which includes the five boroughs of NYC, New Jersey, and parts of Connecticut, upstate New York and Long Island. We've been smack in the middle of the number 1 media market in the world for twenty years, a fact we always took pride in while at the same time always welcomed the enormous responsibility that this opportunity afforded us.

Around the time of our 500th episode, one in which we recruited long-time TV Host Bill Boggs to serve as guest Host and interview me (Mickey Burns) to reminisce about our best memories and highlights over *Profiles'* 500 episode journey, I asked our Photographer Robert Braunfeld, who has been taking photos on and around the set for nearly twenty years: *"Robert, how many photos do you have in your computer from almost two decades with the series"?* He didn't hesitate, and responded: *"I'm not sure, but it's a lot. I'll have to get into my computer and check, but I'll get back to you with a number this evening".* Later that evening the phone rang, it was Robert. *"Hi Robert, thanks for getting back to me. How many photos do you have?"* He quickly responded: *"13,542 photos".*

I couldn't believe he had that many precious photos that chronicled our TV Series.

The next day I was having a conversation with our celebrity publicist Eileen Shapiro and I mentioned to her that our photographer Robert Braunfeld had captured our body of work in 13,542 photos. She laughed and said: *"you have to do a coffee table book"*. I had just released my first book: ***"From Projects to Profiles: A Memoir"*** a few months earlier, and I wasn't sure if I was ready for another major commitment. That book was published by New Haven Publishing LTD., and both Eileen and I loved its CEO Teddie Dahlin. So Eileen said: *"Let me talk to Teddie and get her feelings on moving ahead"*. I responded: *"great, that would be fine"*. The next day I received a text from Eileen, it read: *"Teddy loves the idea and said move forward on the project"*.

I immediately realized that I would be publishing my second book along with my photographer Robert Braunfeld, and I was eager to start thumbing through those 13,542 historic photos with Robert and my Assistant Shani Mitchell. I hope you enjoy the ones we eventually selected.

Host **Mickey Burns** *with* ***Profiles*** *Photographer* **Robert Bruanfield**

PROFILES OVERVIEW

with Mickey Burns

The Award-Winning television series *"Profiles"* with Mickey Burns, filmed in Times Square in the heart of New York City, rocks the Coffee Table world with intimate images in and around the set of Profiles from over the last two decades that features some of the entertainment world's most popular and loved celebrities.

The pages of this book showcase images of iconic Singers, Actors, Musicians, Comedians and Athletes from their appearances on *"Profiles"*. Included are interview quotes and fun facts on the featured celebrities, such as: Smokey Robinson, Susan Lucci, Kenny G, Tony Orlando, Robert Wagner, Misty Copeland, Kandi Burruss, Jesse Ventura, Deepak Chopra, Meatloaf, Mario Lopez, Mayim Bialik, Cheech Marin, Gloria Gaynor, Stacy Keach, Dog The Bounty Hunter, George Foreman, Chrissy Metz, Lou Diamond Phillips, Don McLean, and many more.

"Inside Celebrity Profiles: A Visual Journey" gives readers a tantalizing peek into the world of *"Profiles"* and the process of interviewing celebrities, accompanied by hundreds of never seen before images of the show's famous guests before, during and after their interview. We hope you enjoy your visit!

ABOUT THE HOST

Mickey Burns began Hosting Profiles in 1999. His audience consists of millions of discerning adults, well-educated and successful, who tune in to hear their favorite celebrities from all walks of the show business world engaging in intelligent conversation. Burns has become a favorite among celebrities who after sitting down with him, often comment that it was the best interview that they have ever had.

Mickey hosted over 500 episodes on Profiles that have included many of the top names in the entertainment industry. Mickey Burns television roots can be traced back to Fox 5 News in New York City where he helped produce the "10 O'clock News", "The McCreary Report", and "Sports Extra". In 1987-1988 Mickey was a member of two-Emmy Award winning specials at Fox, "Pro-Life vs. Pro-Choice", and "Domestic Violence".

Profiles Host **Mickey Burns** *opens the show in front of Grand Central Station in the heart of New York*

In the 1990s Mickey Hosted, Anchored and Starred in numerous television programs such: *"Special Edition"*, *"Island View"*, and *"Staten Island Live"* for Time Warner Cable, Inc.

In 1996, Mickey became a founding member and President of Quest Media Entertainment, Inc. In 1999, he created Quest Media's most popular and successful program, **"Profiles"**. A unique talk show showcasing celebrities from all walks of the show business world.

Mickey is a Native of Staten Island, New York. He attended Missouri Valley College on a Football Scholarship. He earned his Bachelor of Science Degree in 1969. The following year he attended Central Missouri State University where he earned his Master of Science Degree.

In 2008, Mickey was honored with the *"Outstanding Alumni Award"* from his Alma Mater Missouri Valley College in Marshall, Missouri. And in 2012, Mickey was presented with an Honorary Doctorate while serving as the Keynote Speaker at the Missouri Valley College Graduation that year.

Mickey is also an Author. In 2019, he released his memoir titled: **"From Projects To Profiles: A Memoir"** published by New Haven Publishing Ltd. Mickey currently lives in Staten Island, New York and continues to Host and Produce the Profiles TV Series.

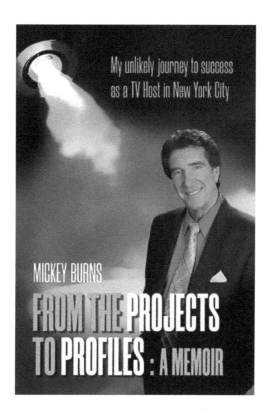

CHAPTER 1

 # THE SINGERS

Over our 500 episode journey we've featured some of the most influential Singers of our time. Each left an indelible mark on their decade and beyond. Interviewing many of them always made me feel like we were chronicling an important piece of music history.

Some of the Singers that have appeared on Profiles include: Ben E. King (*Stand By Me*), Gloria Gaynor (*I Will Survive*), Roberta Flack (*The First Time Ever I Saw Your Face*), B.J. Thomas (*Raindrops Keep Falling On My Head*), Lesly Gore (*It's My Party*), Davy Jones (*Daydream Believer*), CeCe Peniston (*Finally*), Lee Greenwood (*God Bless The USA*), Tommy James (*Mony Mony*), Edgar Winter (*Frankenstein*), Jon Secada (*Just Another Day*), Petula Clark (*Downtown*), Christopher Cross (*Sailing*), Tanya Tucker (*Delta Dawn*), Ronnie Milsap (*Lost In The Fifties Tonight*), KC of KC & The Sunshine Band (*That's The Way I Like It*), Neil Sedaka (*Breaking Up Is Hard To Do*), Aaron Neville (*Tell It Like It Is*), Tony Orlando (*Tie A Yellow Ribbon Round The Old Oak Tree*), Taylor Dayne (*Tell It To My Heart*), Chubby Checker (*The Twist*), Johnny Rivers

(*Secret Agent Man*), Engelbert Humperdick (*After The Lovin'*), Lulu (*To Sir, With Love*), Helen Reddy (*I Am Woman*), Don McLean (*American Pie*), Joan Osborne (*One Of Us*), Melissa Manchester (*Don't Cry Out Loud*), Stephen Bishop (*On & On*), Gino Vannelli (*I Just Wanna Stop*), Bobby Rydell (*Wild One*), Marc Cohn (*Walking In Memphis*), Little Anthony (*Tears On My Pillow*), Rita Coolidge (*Higher and Higher*), Irene Cara (*Fame*), Eddie Money (*Two Tickets to Paradise*), Meat Loaf (*I'd Do Anything For Love*), Charley Pride (*Kiss An Angel Good Mornin'*), Kandi Burruss (*Who Can I Run To*), Charlie Daniels (*The Devil Went Down To Georgia*).

We also had the honor of sitting down with a select group of ***Rock N' Roll Hall Of Fame*** Inductees. They include: *Mick Fleetwood* (1998), *Dion DiMucci* (1989), *Darlene Love* (2011), *Isaac Hayes* (2002), *Sam Moore* (2002), *Bill Medley* (2003), *Darryl "DMC" McDaniels* (2009), *Gregg Rolie* (1998 &2017), *Mary Wilson* (1988), and *Smokey Robinson* (1987).

In this chapter that we've called ***"The Singers"***, we hope to capture in photos some of our most treasured memories and highlights with these Iconic artists.

★★★★ SMOKEY ROBINSON ★★★★

Smokey has written over 400 songs...
When I asked him who his favorite Singer to have recorded one of his compositions was,
without hesitation he responded:
"Marvin Gaye. I would always tell Marvin that he Marvinized my song".
Smokey went on to say:
"What I meant to say is that Marvin always took my music to the next level".

TANYA TUCKER

★★★★ ★★★★

Tanya had her first hit, *Delta Dawn,* in 1972 at the age of thirteen. Tanya is one of the few child stars to venture into adulthood without losing her audience.

★★★★ SAMANTHA FOX ★★★★

English Singer, Songwriter, and former Glamour Model.

At age 16, in 1983 Samantha began appearing topless on page 3 of the British tabloid newspaper *The Sun*. She would go on to be one of the most photographed British women in the 1980s.

In the late 80s she launched a successful music career that spawned several hit records.

★★★★ AARON NEVILLE ★★★★

During our interview I asked Aaron about his array of tattoos and if he had any advice for young people thinking about getting a tattoo?

Laughing, Aaron replied: *"Yeah, they don't come off"*.

★★★★ ENGLEBERT HUMPERDINCK ★★★★

An International Superstar since the mid 1960s with hits such as *"Release Me"* and *"The Last Waltz"*. He has sold more than 140 million records worldwide.

For a decade he worked under the name Jerry Dorsey. In 1965, his manager Gordon Mills suggested a name change to the more interesting Engelbert Humperdinck, borrowed from the 19th century German Composer.

During our interview Mary Wilson said:
"I've worked extremely hard to keep The Supremes legacy alive and well".

Mary went on to say: "I would love to find a permanent home for The Supremes gowns that I have collected from the very beginning".

BILL MEDLEY

Half of the duo of The Righteous Brothers along with Bobby Hatfield. In 1964 they released *"You've Lost That Loving Feeling"* which was produced by Phil Spector's *'Wall of Sound'* recording technique. The song has been described by many critics as one of the best records ever made.

JOAN OSBORNE

★★★★   ★★★★

Singer and Songwriter. Joan's hit recording of *"One of Us"* from her debut album *"Relish"* in 1995 earned her seven Grammy Award Nominations.

★★★★ LEE GREENWOOD ★★★★

Known for his patriotic anthem *"God Bless The U.S.A."* released in 1984, the song then experienced a resurgence during the Gulf War in 1991, and again after the September 11, 2001 attacks.

★★★★ GLORIA GAYNOR ★★★★

During our interview with Gloria she said *"most people thought I was Singing "I Will Survive" to overcome a bad relationship, actually for me it represented my recovering from a serious back injury."*

★★★★ TIFFANY ★★★★

Singer and Teen Idol. Many fans are not aware that Tiffany gave *New Kids On The Block* their first big break when she selected them as her opening act.

★★★★ TONY ORLANDO ★★★★

A native of New York City, Tony has experienced tremendous success as a Singer, Songwriter, Producer and Music Executive. His group *"Tony Orlando and Dawn"* had several hit records in the 1970s, along with a popular television series.

★★★★ DARLENE LOVE ★★★★

In our second interview with Darlene in 2007 she said; *"they better not induct me into the Rock & Roll Hall of Fame after I'm gone."* Thankfully Darlene was inducted into the Hall Of Fame 2011.

★★★★ GINO VANELLI ★★★★

Canadian Singer and Songwriter who had several hit songs in the 1970s and 1980s that included *"I Just Wanna To Stop"* and *"Wild Horses"*. Gino has sold more than 10 million albums worldwide.

★★★★ RONNIE MILSAP ★★★★

One of country music's most popular and influential performers of the 1970s and 1980s.
Ronnie evolved into one of the most successful and versatile Country "Crossover" Singers of his
time. A congenital disorder left him almost completely blind from birth.

★★★★ PETULA CLARK ★★★★

In 1964 Petula recorded *"Downtown"* which catapulted her into international stardom. *"Downtown"* was the first of 15 consecutive Top 40 Hits that Petula achieved in the United States.

★★★★ JOHNNY RIVERS ★★★★

Singer and Songwriter. Who could ever forget *Secret Agent Man*!

Founder of KC & The Sunshine Band, regarding his songwriting prowess KC said; *"I've always felt like the Rodney Dangerfield of songwriting, I never got any respect. However, my songs were no more simplistic than those written by Lennon and McCartney."*

DON McLEAN

In 2017, McLean's classic *"American Pie"* was designated as a cultural treasure by The Library of Congress *"Worthy of Preservation"* in The National Recording Registry as part of America's Patrimony.

★★★★ LATOYA JACKSON ★★★★

During our interview with La Toya, while discussing her brother Michael's passing, La Toya said:
"My first thought when I heard of Michael's death, was not how did he die, but who killed Michael?"

★★ DARRYL DMC McDANIELS ★★

Darryl and Mickey pose with Hollywood Casting Director Sheila Jaffe.

Darryl is a founding member of the Hip Hop Group *RUN DMC*. The group is considered one of the pioneers of Hip Hop culture. *RUN DMC* was inducted into the Rock & Roll Hall of Fame in 2009.

★★★★ FRED SCHNEIDER ★★★★

The frontman and founding member of the popular party band The B-52s since 1977. Their mega hit "Love Shack" is one of the most played karaoke songs around the world.

JUDY COLLINS

★★★★   ★★★★

Singer and songwriter. Judy experienced international success with her recording of Steven Sondheim's *"Send In The Clowns"* from her best-selling 1975 album *"Judith"*.

★★★★ CHARLIE DANIELS ★★★★

Charlie has been on the road with his band *(The Charlie Daniels Band)* for well over 50 years. During our interview Charlie said *"the road devastates some musicians, but I love it. I love waking up in a different motel parking lot every morning."*

During our interview with Davy Jones I asked him *"Have you made a great deal of money as a Monkee?"* He responded *"The money was irrelevant, I can't tell you how great my life has been being part of The Monkees."*

★★★★ GRAHAM NASH ★★★★

Graham is known for his tenor voice and for his songwriting prowess as a member of the English Pop group *The Hollies* and the Folk-Rock Supergroup *Crosby, Stills, and Nash*.

Scottish Singer and Actress. Lulu gained international success with hits such as *"To Sir, With Love"* from the 1967 film of the same name, and with the title song from the 1974 James Bond film *"The Man With The Golden Gun"*.

Lulu with Profiles Make-up Artist Jay Alvear on the set of *Profiles*

Singer and songwriter. Marc's 1991 mega hit *"Walking In Memphis"* from his self-titled debut studio album has been described as an iconic part of the *"Great American Songbook"*. In 1992 Marc won the Grammy Award for Best New Artist.

★★★★ TOMMY JAMES ★★★★

We've had Tommy on as a guest on Profiles three times. During our last interview I mentioned to Tommy that in the beginning his record label CEO Morris Levy told him: *"Tommy, you're about to go on one hell of a ride so buckle-up."* Tommy laughed and said: *"He was absolutely right."*

★★★★ RANDY JONES ★★★★

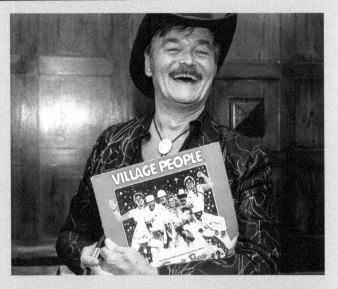

Randy Jones is a Singer and Dancer, he is best known as the Cowboy in the iconic group *"The Village People"*.

Randy with Celebrity Publicist Eileen Shapiro and *Profiles* Host Mickey Burns.

★★★★ TAYLOR DAYNE ★★★★

Taylor Dayne, Singer and Songwriter. A native of Long Island, New York, Taylor rose to fame in 1987 after her debut hit single *"Tell It To My Heart"* climbed to the top of the charts. She followed with an additional Top 10 singles that include: *"Love Will Lead You Back"*, *"Prove Your Love"*, and *"I'll Always Love You"*.

Taylor arrived at the *Profiles* studio with our limousine driver Lydia Loscalco.

★★★★ CHUBBY CHECKER ★★★★

Chubby Checker on the set of Profiles with Bounty Hunter *Duayne "The Dog" Chapman* and *Profiles* Host Mickey Burns.

Chubby demonstrates how to do *"The Twist"* with Actress Alessandra Torresani

Singer Chubby Checker is a Rock N Roll pioneer known for popularizing the dance style known as *"The Twist"*. His song *"The Twist"* became a huge hit in 1960. Chubby followed that with another dance style called *"The Pony"*.

MELBA MOORE

★★★★ ★★★★

Melba Moore shot to superstardom in the 1970s with her debut album *"I Got Love"*. Melba also won a Tony Award (1970) for Best Performance by an actress in a featured role in a Musical *(Purlie)*. During our recent interview with Melba I asked her about the longevity and quality of her singing voice, she responded *"it's better than ever, I treat my voice like an athlete would treat their body"*.

Melba shares with our audience a gift she recieved from Oprah Winfrey
in appreciation of her long and successful career

★★ THE BELLAMY BROTHERS ★★

The Bellamy Brothers are Country Legends having charted 20 number one singles while placing 50 hits on the Country charts overall. The duo had a major crossover hit in 1976 with "Let Your Love Flow" that rose all the way to number one on the Billboard Hot 100 Charts.

MEAT LOAF

Meat Loaf's *"Bat Out of Hell"* trilogy of albums, that include: *"Bat Out of Hell"*, *"Bat Out of Hell II: Back Into Hell"* and *"Bat Out of Hell III: The Monster is Loose"*, has sold more than 50 million albums worldwide.

Incredibly, more than 40 years after their release Meat Loaf's *"Bat Out of Hell"* albums still sell an estimated 200,000 copies each year, making it one of the best selling albums of all-time.

PATTI AUSTIN

Patti Austin is a Grammy Winning R&B, Pop and Jazz Singer. Patti began her show business career when as a four year old she performed at the Apollo Theater.

CHAPTER 2
THE ACTORS

An Actor is a person who portrays a character in a performance. The Actor performs *"In The Flesh"* in the traditional medium of the theatre or in modern media such as film, radio and television. The Actor's interpretation of their role - the art of acting - pertains to the role played, whether based on a real person or fictional character.

Interestingly, in Ancient Greece and Rome, the medieval world, and the time of William Shakespeare, only men could become Actors, and Women's roles were generally played by men or boys. That all changed in the 1600s when women began to appear on stage in England. Women occasionally played the roles of boys or young men.

Acting is certainly one of the oldest professions and can be traced back to as early as 534 B.C. In fact, the theatre in Ancient Rome was a thriving and diverse art form, ranging from festival performances of street theatre, to the staging of situation comedies, to high-style elaborate tragedies. Much has changed since those early days of acting.

Today's actors have theatre, television and film in which to pursue their craft. For many, those who become most successful evolve into our favorite celebrities.

Over our 500 episodes of *Profiles* we've showcased numerous actors that have excelled at just about every form of acting, some on stage, some on television, and others in the movies.

In today's celebrity obsessed society, actors become bigger than life. Our goal on *Profiles* was to peel back the layers and show our viewing audience what the featured actor was like as an individual, what made them tick, and ultimately to unveil the keys that made them successful.

SUSAN LUCCI

When I asked Susan what she hoped her legacy would be, she laughed and said *"I guess I'll always be remembered for Erica Kane"*. A role she portrayed on the ABC Drama *All My Children* from 1970 to 2011.

★★ CHRISTOPHER PLUMMER ★★

When I asked Christopher his thoughts on the Academy Awards he responded:

"it would be better if they just stopped at the nominations. It's not fair to judge an actor in a drama against other actors in a comedy or musical, how can you do that?"

In 2010 Christopher became the oldest actor to win an Oscar at 82 years old for his role in *"All The Money"*.

★★★★ ROBERT WAGNER ★★★★

When I asked Robert about his role as Number Two in the Austin Powers movies, he said:

"I loved doing those films with Mike Myers. However, it's funny that after six decades in films and on television that now I'm known as Number Two".

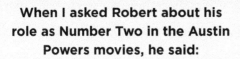

Billy and Mickey pose with Australian Drag Queen and Reality Television personality *Courtney Act*

Multi-talented Star on Broadway and on television, in 2013 Billy won the *Best Actor in a Musical* Award at the 67th Tony Awards for his role as Lola in *Kinky Boots*.

★★★★ CHEECH MARIN ★★★★

Cheech Marin is an accomplished Actor, Comedian, and Activist. He gained enormous popularity in the 1970s and 1980s as part of the comedy team Cheech and Chong.

When I asked Cheech about his role opposite Kevin Costner in *"Tin Cup"* he laughed and said,

"Don Johnson loved my role in that film, shortly after that Don asked me to be his sidekick as Inspector Joe Dominquez in the hit TV series "Nash Bridges".

★★★★ NICKY WHELAN ★★★★

Nicky Whelan is an Australian Actress and Model. After appearing in numerous films and television series since 2004, in 2019 Nicky was cast opposite Bruce Willis in the Blockbuster *"Trauma Center"*. According to Nicky: *"working alongside the screen legend was a real treat"*.

★★★★ SALLY KELLERMAN ★★★★

Sally Kellerman is an Actress and Singer, her accomplished acting career spans over 60 years.

In 1970, Sally earned an Oscar Nomination for Best Actress in a Supporting Role for her portrayal of Margaret "Hot Lips" Houlihan in the hit film M*A*S*H.

In 1986, she starred as Rodney Dangerfield's love interest in the popular film "Back To School".

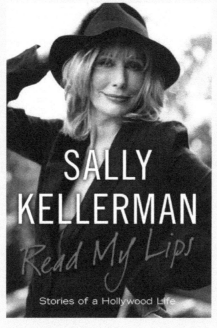

SALLY KELLERMAN
Read My Lips
Stories of a Hollywood Life

★★ LOU DIAMOND PHILLIPS ★★

Actor Lou Diamond Phillips experienced his breakthrough role in 1987 when he starred as Ritchie Valens in the biographical drama *"La Bamba"*.

Lou would later earn an Academy Award Nomination for his role in *"Stand and Deliver"*. In 1996 Phillips made his Broadway debut in the lead role in the revival of *"King and I"*.

Field Producer Raphel Munoz welcomes Lou Diamond Philips to our studio.

Lou poses with Producer Mario Launi, Still Photographer Robert Braunfeld, and Makeup Artist Dana Rodriguez

TIA CARRERE

★★★★  ★★★★

Tia Carrere is an Actress and Singer. When I asked Tia about her earning the role as Cassandra Wong in *Wayne's World* and *Waynes World II* she said:

"I went into that audition feeling that role was perfect for me, especially with my musical background. When I went in I wanted to rock like Pat Benatar.

Other memorable roles include: "True Lies" opposite Arnold Schwarzenegger and as Sydney Fox in the TV series "Relic Hunter".

Tia arrives at *Profiles* for her interview, with limousine driver Lydia Loscalco

DANNY AIELLO

★★★★   ★★★★

Veteran Actor Danny Aiello was nominated for an Academy Award for Best Supporting Actor in 1989 for his portrayal of Salvator "Sal" Frangione in the film *"Do The Right Thing"*. Other notable roles include: *"Moonstruck"*, *"The Godfather Part II"*, and *"Once Upon A Time In America"*.

We lost Danny in December of 2019, he was 86 years old.

CHRISSY METZ

Actress and Singer Chrissy Metz is best known for her role as Kate Pearson in the hit NBC television series *"This Is Us"*, which earned her nominations for a Primetime Emmy Award and two Golden Globe Awards. During our interview with Chrissy she said, *"I thought success and joy weren't coming for me"*. She went on to say, *"they were inside me all along"*.

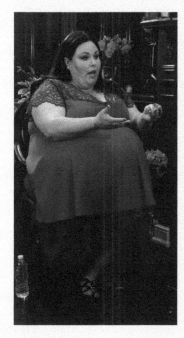

Chrissy chats with Videographer Caitlin Tepper on the set of *Profiles*

★★ DUANE DOG CHAPMAN ★★

Duane Dog Chapman is a reality TV Star and former Bail Bondsman. In 2004, the A&E network gave him his own series *"Dog The Bounty Hunter"*. During our interview, while discussing his profession, The Dog said, *"If the cops weren't so busy chasing criminals all over the place there wouldn't be a need for bounty hunters. However, unfortunately that's not the case"*.

The Dog poses with the *Guardian Angels* in Times Square after his *Profiles* interview

MING-NA WEN

★★★★   ★★★★

Since 2013 Actress Ming-Na Wen has been starring as Melinda May in the ABC drama series *"Agents of S.H.I.E.L.D."*. Ming Na is also a Disney Princess for voicing Mulan in the animated musical action films *"Mulan"* (1998) and *"Mulan II"* (2004).

MAYIM BIALIK

★★★★   ★★★★

Mayim Bialik is an Actress, Neuroscientist and Author. Mayim literally grew up on television playing the character of *Blossom* in the popular NBC sitcom. In recent years she starred as Neurobiologist Amy Fowler on the hit CBS sitcom *"The Big Bang Theory"*.

BURT YOUNG

★★★★  ★★★★

Field Producer
Ralph Munoz
talking cigars with
Burt Young

When I asked Burt to explain the enormous success of the Rocky franchise he responded
"Rocky gets knocked down time and time again and always gets up.
He's every man who tries and refuses to give up".

Senior Producer & Editor Monina Montenegro
gets a hug from Burt.

★★★★ ERNEST BORGNINE ★★★★

We had Oscar winner Ernest Borgnine on Profiles when he was 94 years old.

When I asked him how he stays so mentally sharp he said, *"every morning I get up and do crossword puzzles... exercise for the mind!"*

KEVIN SORBO

★★★★   ★★★★

Kevin Sorbo with Profiles Host Mickey Burns and *Tae Bo* founder Billy Blanks

Kevin Sorbo started his show business career as a Model and worked in television commercials. His breakthrough as an actor came in 1994 when he was cast as the Ancient Greek Mythology Demigod *Hercules* making him internationally famous.

★★★★ LESLIE CARON ★★★★

When I asked Leslie about her starring role in the 1958 film *"Gigi"* which won the Academy Award for Best Picture that year, she said *"Gigi was the most perfect musical ever made"*.

In 2007 Leslie won an Emmy Award for Outstanding Guest Actress in a drama series portraying a rape victim on *"Law & Order: Special Victim's Unit"*.

★★★★ DANICA McKELLER ★★★★

Danica McKeller is an Actress, Mathematics Author, and Education Advocate. She became famous playing Winnie Cooper in the Award winning TV series *"The Wonder Years"* from 1988-1993.

Most recently, Danica has starred in numerous films on the Hallmark Channel.

Profiles Makeup Artist Jay Alvear putting hair & make-up finishing touches for Danica's interview.

★★★★ BRUCE CAMPBELL ★★★★

Actor Bruce Campbell poses with the *Profiles* Crew

Bruce Campbell has more than earned his moniker as the "King of the B-Movies" his starring roles include Ash in Sam Raimi's *"Evil Dead"* and *"Evil Dead II"* film series.

Regarding how movie making has evolved Bruce said *"I ascertained that with the advances in technology a filmmaker can produce a movie for under 10 thousand dollars"*.

★★★★ ERIC ROBERTS ★★★★

During our interview I asked Eric, brother of Actress Julia Roberts, if he learned anything from his early "wild days" in Hollywood, he said:

"those people who I treated poorly and with disrespect will eventually rise up from the ashes and get even, and they have."

Eric went on to say *"the lesson here is be nice to everyone"*.

Eric Roberts arrives for his appearance on *Profiles* with his wife Eliza

Broadcast Journalist Marlie Hall gets a kiss from Eric

TATYANA ALI

Tatyana Ali made her acting breakthrough in 1990 when she was cast as Ashley Banks on the popular television sitcom *"The Fresh Prince of Bel-Air"*, a role she played throughout the series' entire run from 1990-1996.

★★★★ JOHN O'HURLEY ★★★★

John O'Hurley is an Actor, Comedian, and Television Personality. John is best known for his role as J. Peterman on the NBC sitcom *"Seinfeld"*.

He also hosted the game show *"Family Feud"* from 2006 to 2010.

Field Producer Ralph Munoz welcomes John O'Hurley to *Profiles*

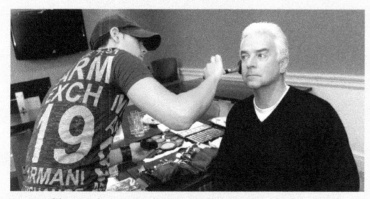

Profiles Makeup Artist Jay Alvear gets John ready for his *Profiles* interview

DAVID ZAYAS

★★★★ ★★★★

Actor David Zayas is best known for his roles as Angel Batista on Showtime's hit series *"Dexter"*, and as Enrique Morales on the HBO Prison Drama *"OZ"* and most recently as Sal Maroni on the FOX series *"Gotham"*.

Getting ready for our next roles as *"Hitmen"*

★★★★ MICHAEL IMPERIOLI ★★★

Profiles team welcomes Actor Michael Imperioli to the set of Profiles

Michael Imperioli is an Actor, Director, and Author. He became famous for his role as Christopher Moltisanti on the mega-hit HBO series "The Sopranos" for which he won the Primetime Emmy Award for Outstanding Supporting Actor in a Drama Series in 2004.

Patricia Velasquez is a Model and Actress born in Maracaibo, Venezuela. In the 1990's Patricia appeared on the covers of *Vogue* and *Bazaar*, she was also featured in several issues of the annual *Sports Illustrated Swimsuit Editions*. Her acting breakthrough came in 1999 when she was cast as Anck Su Namun in the film *"The Mummy"* and its 2001 sequel *"The Mummy Returns"*.

Patricia with Publicist
Rob Goldstone

★★★ JOHNATHAN SCHAECH ★★★

Johnathon Schaech is an Actor, Writer and Producer. Although Johnathon has appeared in over 60 featured films, our favorite is his role as Jimmy Mattingly in the film *"That Thing You Do"* directed by Tom Hanks.

Profiles team on the set with Actor Johnathon Schaech

Johnathon with Broadway Actress Luba Mason and Host Mickey Burns

★★★★ CAROL CHANNING ★★★★

On the set of *Profiles* in 2005 with Carol Channing and her Husband Harry Kullijian

Carol Channing is a legend of Broadway and Musicals. Carol starred in a remarkable 4,500 performances in her role as Dolly in the production of *"Hello Dolly"* for which she won the Tony Award for *Best Actress in a Musical*. She later donated a dress she wore in *"Hello Dolly"* to the National Museum of American History at the Smithsonian Institution.

Carol arrives for her *Profiles* interview with limousine driver Lydia Loscalzo *(limos by lydia)*

CHAPTER 3
★★★★ ## THE MUSICIANS **★★★★**

According to Webster, a *musician* is a person who plays a musical instrument or is musically talented. Without a doubt the key word here is talented. Over the years we've had some extraordinary musicians as guests on *Profiles*. Many have risen to the top in their respective fields, specific instruments and talents.

Some that come to mind include:
Kenny G (saxophone), ***Lang Lang*** (piano),
Sheila E (percussion), ***Carl Palmer*** (drums),
Chuck Mangione (flugelhorn),
Malina Moye (guitar), and
Gregg Rolie (keyboards)
just to mention a few.

In 2015, we had musician ***Kenny G*** as a guest on Profiles. At the time he was passing through New York City on a promotional media tour for his seventeenth studio album titled: *"Brazilian Nights"*. It was also his second Bossa Nova Album.

Kenny walked into our studio carrying his saxophone. I thought to myself, if we can get him to play a little bit during the interview it would be a really special experience. About ten minutes into our interview, I asked him to do exactly that. He then enthusiastically cooperated. Kenny took his saxophone out of its case and began to play some smooth jazz that he's become famous for.

I then asked Kenny G to explain some of the discipline of his instrument. In layman's terms, *"Kenny tell us how your instrument works"*. Kenny proceeded to give us a saxophone tutorial which I found fascinating. Kenny then said: *"Mickey, this is the saxophone I got while playing in my high school band"*. He went on to say: *"It costs me about 300 dollars, today this model would cost about three thousand dollars"*. Kenny went on to explain that he's used this saxophone from his high school days on just about every recording he's ever made.

KENNY G

Saxophonist Kenny G is one of the best-selling artists of all time with global sales totaling more than seventy five million records worldwide. A native of Seattle, Washington Kenny started playing the saxophone at 10 years old when he heard a performance on the Ed Sullivan Show.

CARL PALMER

★★★★ ★★★★

Legendary Drummer Carl Palmer poses with Singer Theresa Sareo on the set of *Profiles*.

Carl Palmer is an English Drummer and Percussionist. He is one of the most respected Rock Drummers to emerge from the 1960s. Carl was the Drummer for two highly successful bands, *"Emerson, Lake and Palmer"* and then *"ASIA"*.
He was inducted into the Modern Drummer Hall of Fame in 1989.

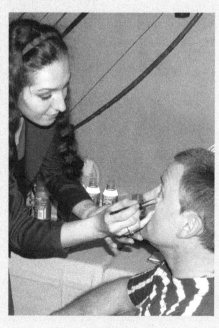

Carl gives Field Producer
Ralph Munoz a pair of
autographed drumsticks.

Lang Lang is a Chinese concert Pianist who has performed with elite orchestras worldwide. Lang Lang has evolved into one of the world's most influential and committed Musicians.

Field Producer Ralph Munoz poses with Lang Lang
after signing his book *Journey of a Thousand Miles: My Story*

SHEILA E

Often referred to as *"The Queen of Percussion"*, since the 1970s, Sheila E has performed with Lionel Richie, Marvin Gaye, Diana Ross and Prince. In 2014 she released her successful autobiography: *"Beat of My Own Drum"*.

Sheila E gracefully participates in the Ice Bucket Challenge with *Profiles* Host Mickey Burns

★★★★ MALINA MOYE ★★★★

Malina Moye is a Singer-Songwriter and Guitarist. She is widely recognized as one of the first African American left-handed, upside-down female Guitarists.

Malina is often referred to as *the female Jimi Hendrix.*

GREGG ROLIE

Gregg Rolie is one of Rock's premiere keyboardists. He is also a two-time *Rock n' Roll Hall of Fame* Inductee, having been inducted both as a member of *Santana* in 1998, and as a member of *Journey* in 2017. Since 2012, Gregg has toured as a member of *Ringo Starr and his All Star Band*.

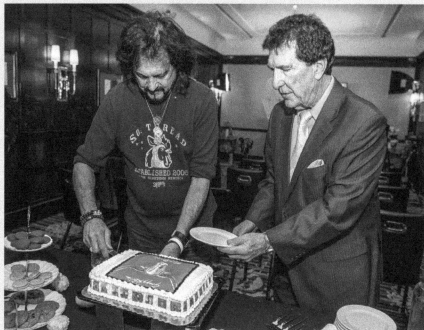

Gregg cuts the cake in celebration of his latest album release *"Sonic Ranch"*.

★★★★ TITO PUENTE JR ★★★★

Tito Puente Jr is a Bandleader and the son of famous Mambo Musician Tito Puente.

During our interview Tito said: *"my mission is to keep my fathers' legacy alive and well by presenting his music in my performances and recordings".*

Tito on the set of *Profiles* with his sister, Fox Meteorologist Audrey Puente, and *Profiles* Executive Producer and former Fox Anchorman Bill McCreary

STEVE JONES

★★★★ ★★★★

Steve Jones is an English Rock Guitarist, best known as a founding member of the legendary British band *The Sex Pistols*. Growing up in Class-Ruled Britain, *The Sex Pistols'* popularity exploded through their music and lyrics, that taunted and ridiculed the establishment.

TONY IOMMI

Tony Iommi is a Guitarist and founding member of the heavy metal band *Black Sabbath*. When I asked Tony about the band's name, he said:

"We were originally known as Earth, however that wasn't working out too well. So I borrowed Black Sabbath from an old Boris Karloff movie poster I had seen."

Host Mickey Burns welcomes Guitar legend Tony Iommi of *Black Sabbath* to the set of *Profiles*

★★★★ EDDIE PALMIERI ★★★★

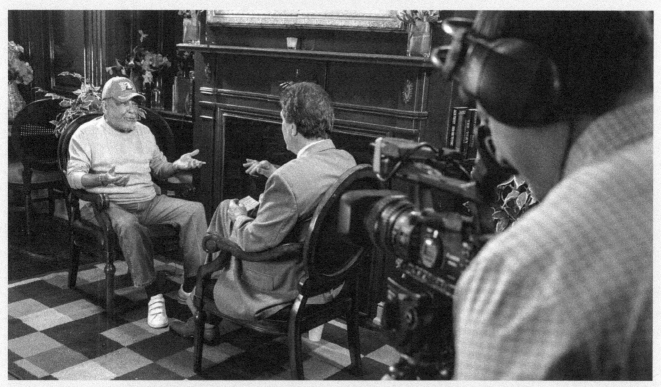

Eddie Palmieri is one of the finest pianists of the past 60 years.
He is a legend as a Band Leader, Arranger, and Composer of Salsa and Latin Jazz.
Mr. Palmieri is the recipient of nine Grammy Awards.

★★★★ FELICIA COLLINS ★★★★

Felicia Collins is best known for her work on the CBS program *Late Show with David Letterman* as the Guitarist in the CBS orchestra. During her interview Felicia said: *"I always considered my experience as part of the CBS orchestra as one of the best jobs in show business"*.

Television Legal Expert Jack Ford and Host Mickey Burns pose with Felicia Collins on the set of *Profiles*

★★★★ KENNY ARONOFF ★★★★

Kenny Aronoff is a Drummer who has worked with many bands both live and in the studio. He was the Drummer for *John Mellencamp*'s Band from 1982-1986. Kenny also shared the stage with *Ringo Starr* and *Paul McCartney* for a tribute to *The Beatles*. Afterwards Kenny told Ringo: *"you're the reason I'm playing drums, and you're the reason I decided to be a musician"*.

★★ NARADA MICHAEL WALDEN ★★

Narada Michael Walden is a Musician and Record Producer who has produced recordings for *Aretha Franklin, Patti Austen, Lionel Richie, Mariah Carey, Whitney Houston* and many more.
He has been nominated for eight Grammy Awards, winning three.
Narada is currently the Drummer for *Journey*.

Bo Bice is a Singer and Musician who was named the Runner-Up against Carrie Underwood in the fourth season of *American Idol*. Bo later worked as the lead singer of *"Blood Sweat & Tears"*.

★★★★ CARMINE APPICE ★★★★

Carmine Appice is one of Rock's premiere Drummers who first came to prominence as the Drummer with the late 1960s band *Vanilla Fudge*. In the 1970s & 1980s Carmine toured as *Rod Stewart*'s Drummer. According to Appice: *"Rod is the greatest Frontman ever in Rock 'n' Roll"*.

Carmine chats with Singer Bobby Rydell
on the set of *Profiles*

CHAPTER 4
★★★★ **THE COMEDIANS** ★★★★

I always looked forward to having Comedians as guests on *Profiles*. **Going into these interviews I felt that Comedians were unpredictable, which for the most part offered unlimited potential for entertaining episodes.**

My expectation prior to interviewing Comedians was that they would naturally do their best to be funny during the process. Interestingly, that was not always the case - yes, they sprinkled in some funny, but for the most part what I constantly got were Comedians who wanted to talk about their lives and what made them click. As it turned out, it was great to peel back the layers and to get to know these talented people beyond the jokes and comedy skits.

We had **Joan Rivers** on *Profiles* twice, each interview was extremely memorable. Ironically, during the second interview we talked in length about her interest and history with plastic surgery. As she said during that interview: *"Better to have a new face coming out of an old car, than an old face coming out of a new car"*.

One day in 2006, I was working in our office when the phone rang, my assistant picked up the call then turned to me and said it's **David Brenner**, he wants to talk to you. I immediately

took the call, which went like this: *"Hi Mickey, it's David Brenner. I caught your show the other night and loved it. If you're interested I'd love to come on as a guest."* I almost fell off of my chair. I quickly responded: *"Are you kidding, it would be an honor to have you on the show, I've been a big fan for a long time - let's make this happen."* We then both looked at our schedules and booked David to appear on the show a couple of weeks later.

In 2001, we were attempting to book *Saturday Night Live* Alumni **Joe Piscopo** on *Profiles*. It wasn't easy, at the time he was a single Dad doing his best to raise and care for his four children.

So, rather than conduct the interview in our Times Square Studio, Joe suggested we do the interview from his home in Western New Jersey. We agreed, and in early Spring of 2009 we headed off to Joe's home. Once there, we set up in Joe's living room and began our interview. What I learned that day was that as accomplished as Joe's professional career was, he also had his priorities in order. He extensively verbalized on how raising his children was without a doubt the most important aspect of his life.

JOAN RIVERS

★★★★ ★★★★

Joan Rivers was a legendary Comedian, Actress, Writer, Producer, Author and Television Host.

We had Joan on *Profiles* twice, each time she left us with an unforgettable experience.

In 2017, *Rolling Stone* ranked her sixth on the list of 50 Best Stand-Up Comedians of all time.

★★ SEBASTIAN MANISCALCO ★★

In 2019 Superstar Stand-Up Comedian Sebastian Maniscalco performed four back to back, sold out shows in Madison Square Guard, totaling 73,000 fans in the audience over one weekend. The massively popular comic said: *"I believe there's an audience that's been underserved in the comedy world - family observational humor you can enjoy with your grandkids, grandmother and everybody in between. My material is non-political, good-natured and not at all mean-spirited. I don't feel that people want to hear that when they go out for the evening"*.

DAVID BRENNER

★★★★   ★★★★

David Brenner was a Stand-Up Comedian, Actor and Author. He was also the Writer, Director and Producer of 115 Television Documentaries. After making his national debut in 1971 on *The Tonight Show Starring Johnny Carson*, he became the show's most frequent guest with 158 appearances. David would also serve as Guest Host for Johnny Carson 75 times.

★★★★ FRANK CALIENDO ★★★★

Frank Caliendo is a Comedian and Impressionist, best known for his impersonations on *MAD TV* and as the In-House Prognosticator for *Fox NFL Sunday*. His impressions of former NFL Coach John Madden are legendary. Additionally, Frank's impression of President George W. Bush earned him an invitation to perform at the 2006 *Radio-Television Correspondents Dinner*.

★★★★ MARILYN MICHAELS ★★★★

On the set of *Profiles* with Mariyln Michaels, Host Mickey Burns and Marilyn's son, Author Mark Wilk

Marilyn Michaels is a Comedian, Singer, Actress, Impressionist, Author, Painter and Composer. In the early 1970s, Marilyn starred as the only female performer in the Emmy-Nominated ABC Comedy Series *"The Kopykats"*. In 2018, Marilyn along with her son Mark Wilk released a humorous biography *"How Not To Cook For The Rest Of Your Life"*.

Marilyn poses with her painting of Elizabeth Taylor (Cleopatra)

★★★★ JAMES MURRAY ★★★★

Profiles Team welcomes *Impractical Jokers'* James Murray to *Profiles*

A native of Staten Island, New York, James Murray is a member of *The Tenderloins*, a comedy troupe also consisting of Sal Vulcano, Joe Gatto and Brian Quinn. Since 2011, James has been starring on the enormously popular TV Series *"Impractical Jokers"*.

During our *Profiles* interview, James said: *"I thought this interview was going to be a prank for Impractical Jokers, I kept waiting for the camera crews to appear"*.

★★★★ LISA LAMPANELLI ★★★★

Lisa Lampanelli is a Comedian and Actress. She began her career doing Stand-Up in New York City Comedy Clubs in the early 1980's. In 2008, she produced her first one hour special for HBO.

Lisa also appeared as a contestant on *"The Celebrity Apprentice 5"* where she made it to the final four.

TIM CONWAY

Tim Conway was a Comedian and Actor who appeared in more than 100 TV Shows from 1966-2012. Most notably for his role as Ensign Parker in the TV Situation Comedy *"McHales Navy"* and as a regular cast member on the popular Comedy Series *"The Carol Burnett Show"*.

JOE PISCOPO

Joe Piscopo is a Comedian, Actor, Musician and Radio Talk Show Host. Joe is best known for his work in the 1980s on *Saturday Night Live*, where he played a variety of recurring characters. In January 2014, Joe began hosting *"The Answer"* on AM 970 radio in New York City.

★★★★ PABLO FRANCISCO ★★★★

Pablo Francisco is a Comedian who started his career doing Improv in Tempe, Arizona.

In the early 2000s he toured as part of *"The Three Amigos"* with Carlos Mencia and Freddy Soto.

Pablo is recognized for his spot on impressions of famous people including: Jackie Chan, Aaron Neville, Arnold Schwarzenegger, Howard Stern, Michael J. Fox and Danny Glover just to mention a few.

Comedian Pablo Fancisco arrives on the set for his *Profiles* Interview

RICH LITTLE

Rich Little is a Canadian Impressionist who has been nicknamed *"The Man of a Thousand Voices"*. Beginning in the 1960s, Rich has appeared on numerous TV Shows and Specials. In the 1970s, he was a regular cast member on the popular ABC series *"The Kopykats"*.

In 2007, Rich hosted *The White House Correspondents Dinner.*

Producer Mario Launi gets ready to mic up Rich for his *Profiles* interview

Chuck Barris was a Game Show Creator, Comedian, Producer and Host. In 1976, Chuck created and hosted *"The Gong Show"* on NBC. He also created *"The Dating Game"* and *"Newlywed Game"*, both were enormously popular. At the end of our *Profiles* interview I asked Chuck what he hoped his legacy would be? With a big smile he replied: *"I want it written on my tombstone Gonged At Last"*.

Pat Cooper is a Comedian who has been extremely popular since the 1960s. Born and raised in Brooklyn, New York, he often made reference to his Italian heritage in his Stand-Up comedy routines. During his illustrious career Pat often appeared on the same shows as Frank Sinatra, Tony Bennett, Bobby Darin, Ella Fitzgerald and Sammy Davis Jr., just to mention a few.

Pat Cooper on the set of Profiles with New York Post Entertainment Correspondent Michael Starr

CHAPTER 5
THE ATHLETES

As a former Football and Baseball player I always loved having Athletes on Profiles. I understood what it takes to rise to the top of their sport. Athletes live their lives playing and performing under intense pressure. So I was fully aware that for them to sit across from me for an interview was soft steak.

In 2007, we booked former Heavyweight Champion **George Foreman** on *Profiles*. At the time all I could think about was his 1974 fight with Muhammad Ali, which was famously named, *"The Rumble in the Jungle"*. A fight that Foreman lost, after getting knocked out by Ali in the 8th round. The fight was watched that day by an estimated television audience of one billion viewers worldwide, becoming the world's most watched live television broadcast at the time, and I was one of them.

George entered our studio on the day of the interview impeccably dressed in a perfectly tailored white suit, he looked like a million

bucks. Of course, we talked about *"The Rumble in the Jungle"*, surprisingly George said he thought he was drugged during the fight and he felt someone had slipped something into his water. Ultimately, George admitted that on that night Ali was the better fighter.

Mid-way into the interview we switched gears and began discussing his career as a businessman. As the spokesperson for *The George Foreman Grill,* which has sold over 100 million units, George has earned over 200 million dollars from his endorsement, substantially more than he ever earned as a boxer. So I asked George: *"What's been the key to your business success?"* George smiled and said: *"Mickey, a good business deal is only a good one when both parties are happy."*

Other Athletes we've had on *Profiles* include: Olympians, NBA Greats, Pro Baseball Legends, NFL Stars, Coaches and Fitness Experts.

All created memorable *Profiles* episodes.

★★★★ KRISTI YAMAGUCHI ★★★★

Kristi Yamaguchi is a Champion Figure Skater who was a 1992 Olympic Gold Medal Winner, a two-time World Champion (1991 & 1992) and the 1992 United States Champion.

In 2008, Kristi became the Celebrity Champion in the sixth season of *"Dancing With The Stars"*.

★★★★ TAI BABILONIA ★★★★

Tai Babilonia is a former Pair Figure Skater.

Together with Randy Gardner she won the 1979 *World Figure Skating Championships* and five *U.S. Figure Skating Championships* (1976-1980).

Tai and Randy qualified for the 1976 and 1980 Winter Olympics.

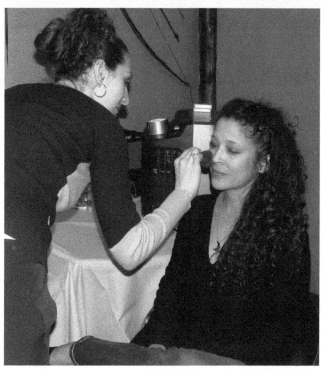

Tai arrives for her *Profiles* interview with Limo Driver Lydia Loscalo

★★★★ GEORGE FOREMAN ★★★★

George Foreman is a two-time World Heavyweight Champion and an Olympic Gold Medalist. George finished his Professional Boxing Career with a record of 76 wins and 5 loses. Of his 76 wins, 68 came by way of knockout. In 2002, George was named one of the *25 Greatest Fighters of the past 80 years* by *The Ring* Magazine.

George signs a photo for Female Professional Boxing Champion Maureen Shea

Profiles Photographer Robert Braunfeld gets to meet the champ!

BILLY BLANKS

★★★★   ★★★★

Welcoming Fitness Guru Billy Blanks to the set of *Profiles*

Billy Blanks is a Fitness Guru, Martial Artist, Actor and the creator of *"Tae Bo"* exercise program. In the late 1990s, Billy's *"Tae Bo Workout Routine"* swept around the world, and propelled him into one of the world's most recognizable and biggest selling fitness trainers.

JEANETTE LEE

★★★★ ★★★★

Getting a lesson from the *Black Widow*

Jeanette "Black Widow" Lee
is a former Professional Pool Player.

The formerly Ranked #1 player in the world, Jeanette earned her nickname *"The Black Widow"* by her friends because, in spite of her sweet demeanor, she was far from that at the pool table where she would consistently eat people alive.

In 2007, she was Ranked #4 in *Pool and Billiard Magazine's Top 20 Favorite Players* Poll.

EARL MONROE

Earl "The Pearl" Monroe meets former Supermodel Kathy Ireland on the set of *Profiles*

Earl "The Pearl " Monroe is a former Professional Basketball Star who played for two teams, The Baltimore Bullets and The New York Knicks. Both teams have retired Monroe's number. His flashy style of play is legendary. During our *Profiles* interview, I asked The Pearl to explain some of his famous moves, he replied: *"I can't explain the things I've done on the court, in fact, sometimes I had to go back to the videotape to see exactly what I did, and how I did it".*

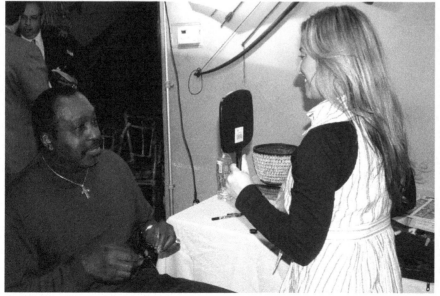

WALT FRAZIER

Walt "Clyde" Frazier is a former Professional Basketball All-Star.

During his career he was a floor general while leading the New York Knicks to the franchises' only two championships (1970 and 1973). Upon his retirement from the NBA, Frazier went into broadcasting. He is currently a Color Commentator for the *Knicks* telecast on the *MSG* Network.

Walt shares his two
NBA Championship rings
with our audience

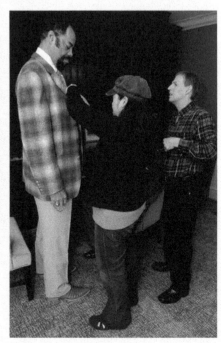

RON SWOBODA

Profiles Team welcomes former New York Mets Star Ron Swoboda to *Profiles*

Ron Swoboda is a former Professional Baseball Player and a member of the 1969 *"Miracle Mets"*. In game 4 of the 1969 World Series, playing right field, Swoboda made a spectacular catch that saved the game for the Mets. Today, a photograph of Swoboda stretched almost horizontally, making his iconic catch, is embedded in the right field entrance gate of City Field.

★★★★ KEITH HERNANDEZ ★★★★

Keith Hernandez is a former *Major League* First Baseman who played for the *St. Louis Cardinals* and the *New York Mets*. Hernandez was a five-time All-Star who shared the 1979 *National League MVP* Award with Willie Stargell, and won two *World Series* Titles, one each with the Cardinals and Mets. Currently, Keith is a baseball commentator serving as an analyst for *Mets Television Broadcast* on the SNY Network.

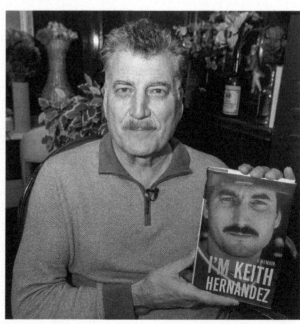

RON DARLING

★★★★ ★★★★

Profiles Crew welcomes former New York Mets Star Ron Darling to the set of *Profiles*

Ron Darling is a former starting Pitcher in Major League Baseball who played for the *Montreal Expos, Oakland Athletics* and The World Champion 1986 *New York Mets*.
Since his retirement from baseball, Ron works as a Color Commentator for National Baseball Coverage on *TBS*, as well as for *NY Mets* on the *SNY* Network.

★★★ DOMINIQUE MOCEANU ★★★

Dominique Moceanu is a retired World Class Gymnast and Author.
She was a member of the Gold Medal-Winning United States Women's Gymnastic team
known as *"The Magnificent 7"* at the 1996 Summer Olympics in Atlanta, Georgia.

CHAPTER 6
★★★★ **THE INFLUENCERS** ★★★★

Celebrity Influencers are a powerful force to be reckoned with when it comes to marketing, creating a brand or even entering politics.

For example, *Deepak Chopra* has written nearly one hundred books while evolving into one of the world's leading authorities in the field of Holistic Medicine. Along his journey he has won legions of followers.

Kathy Ireland transformed her celebrity as a Supermodel into the world of business when she created *Kathy Ireland Worldwide,* one of the most successful brand marketing companies in the world.

And *Jesse Ventura* converted his celebrity as a star wrestler in the WWF into a career as an actor and prolific author. In 1998, Jesse became the Governor of Minnesota.

I'll never forget having former Talk Show Host *Dick Cavett* on the show. He inspired a generation of Talk Show Hosts, myself included, on how to conduct a professional interview. His conversational style was unique and intelligent. During our interview Mr. Cavett reminded me: *"Mickey, always be yourself"*.

Having *Maya Dr. Angelou* on *Profiles* was a thrill of a lifetime. Prior to the interview, all I could think about was my concern that I was in way over my head. However, Dr. Angelou never made me feel that way. Instead she exemplified her wit, grace and thought-provoking intelligence by giving me an interview that I will always treasure.

In this chapter, we showcase just some of the celebrity influencers that have appeared as guests on *Profiles*. All have many fans and gigantic followings.

★★★★ DEEPAK CHOPRA ★★★★

Deepak Chopra is a prominent figure in the *New Age* movement. His books, of which he's written nearly one hundred, have made him one of the best known figures in alternative medicine.

Mr. Chopra increased his following enormously in the early 1990s when he became a frequent guest on *The Oprah Winfrey Show*.

DICK CAVETT

★★★★ ★★★★

Dick Cavett is a former Talk Show Host who set the bar high for intelligent conversation on television. Mr. Cavett was extremely popular for his in-depth discussions.

Senior Producer & Editor
Monina Montenegro gets a hug
from Mr. Cavett

Profiles Limo Driver Lydia Loscalo arrives to the set of *Profiles*
with TV Talk Show Legend Dick Cavett

KATHY IRELAND

Kathy Ireland is a former Supermodel turned author and entrepreneur. Back in the 1980s and 1990s, Kathy appeared in 13 consecutive *Sports Illustrated* swimsuit issues. In 1993, she founded *Kathy Ireland Worldwide*, a brand marketing company. This venture made her one of the wealthiest former models in the world. As a result of her business career, by 2015 she had earned a personal fortune of approximately $20 million dollars.

★★★★ DR. MAYA ANGELOU ★★★★

Dr. Maya Angelou was one of America's Greatest Poets. She published seven autobiographies, three books of essays and several books of poetry.

Dr. Angelou received dozens of awards and more than 50 honorary degrees.

PETE HAMMILL

★★★★ **PETE HAMMILL** ★★★★

Pete Hamill was a columnist and editor for the *New York Post* and the *New York Daily News*. As a columnist, he saw to capture the flavors of New York City's Politics, Sports, and Crime. No one knew or represented New York City better than Pete Hamill, who passed away in August 2020.

★★★★ **GRETCHEN CARLSON** ★★★★

Gretchen Carlson is a former *Miss America* (1989) from Minnesota. Gretchen later became an accomplished Journalist, Author, and Television Commentator. In 2017, she was named one of *Time* Magazine's *100 Most Influential People in the World*.

JESSE VENTURA

★★★★ ★★★★

Jesse Ventura is the former Governor of Minnesota, Actor, Author and retired Professional Wrestler.

After leaving the military, Jesse embarked on a Professional Wrestling career from 1975-1986, taking the ring name *Jesse "The Body" Ventura*. In addition to wrestling, Ventura also embarked in an acting career. In 1987, he starred in the hit film *"Predator"* opposite Arnold Schwarzenegger.

★★★★ MISTY COPELAND ★★★★

In 2016, Misty made history by becoming the first African-American woman promoted to Principal Dancer in the 75 year history of the *American Ballet Theater*. Also, in 2015, Misty was named one of the *"100 Most Influential People in the World"* by *Time* Magazine.

★★★★ ANDREW ZIMMERN ★★★★

Andrew Zimmern is a world-renowned Chef and Television Host.

His award-winning TV Series *"Bizarre Foods"* on The Travel Channel recently celebrated its 12th season.

Andrew's ultimate mission is to promote cultural acceptance, tolerance and understanding through food.

★★★★ KANDI BURRUSS ★★★★

Kandi Burruss is the consummate show business role model, having excelled as a Singer, Songwriter, Actress, Businesswoman and Television Personality.

Kandi spent most of the 1990s as a member of the popular female group *Xscape*. Since 2009, she's been one of the stars in the Bravo reality television series *The Real Housewives of Atlanta*.

Most recently, she was the winner of season three of the Fox Competition series *The Masked Singer*.

CHAPTER 7
EPILOGUE

In January of 2020 Profiles celebrated its 500th episode. It's been quite a journey to say the least.

In March of 2020, the *Covid-19* pandemic hit, and New York City became the epicenter for this horrible and deadly disease. By late March we found ourselves quarantined in our homes. Manhattan came to a standstill, the streets became barren of people, restaurants and stores were shut tight. Not being able to produce new *Profiles* episodes at least afforded us the opportunity to complete our coffee table book, a visual journey of highlights from our 500 episodes.

As we were putting this book together, I often reflected on how fortunate I've been to have had the opportunity to sit down with so many legends and icons, and in doing so, I had the privilege of sharing the highlights of their lives and careers. In most cases, I walked away from these interviews feeling that I learned many life lessons that will remain with me always.

Additionally, I've made a lot of new friends along the way whom I treasure. For instance, I had **Tony Orlando** on *Profiles* twice. Perhaps because

we were both born and raised in New York City, we easily clicked. When I completed my first book in 2019, *"From The Projects To Profiles: A Memoir"* I sent Tony a text message asking him if he would be so kind to write a blurb for the book's back cover. To my delight, within fifteen minutes Tony's blurb was right at the top in my email inbox. That's just one of the many special friendships I've formed doing this show.

The pandemic gave us all a greater appreciation of what we had and what we've all been doing for the past 20 years. Actually, it's a time for new beginnings, new hopes, new goals and, most importantly, the opportunity to continue to do what we all love so much, and that is to produce the *Profiles* TV Series from Times Square in the heart of New York City.

Thank you for sharing the first part of our journey with us - in photos!

Mickey Burns

★★★★ ACKNOWLEDGEMENTS ★★★★

Special thanks to the Photographers who captured two decades of memories on the set of *Profiles*, they include: Robert Braunfeld, Jeff Smith, Georgine Benvenuto and Billy Hess. Your images are priceless!

I would like to thank my partner Edwina Frances Martin for her undying love and support. Arick Wierson, Diane Petzke and Janet Choi - General Managers at the NYC Media Network. Mike McKenna and Creative Director, Roland LeBreton.

To NYC Council Member Debi Rose (D) of the 49th District serving the North Shore of Staten Island for her guidance, friendship and support. Former Staten Island Borough President Ralph Lamberti for your lifetime of guidance and friendship. Former Fox Anchor Bill McCreary for mentoring me from the start. Wayne Miller and Al Lambert for always being there.

The *Profiles* Team: Gary Humienny, Mario Launi, Michael "Disco Mike" Park, Justin Clouden, Shani Mitchell, Masieneth Ouk, Jorge Guzman Cruz, Rafael Munoz, Caitlin Tepper, Marlie Hall, Desi Sanchez, Laura Ameruso, Erica Martinez, and Jay Alvear for helping make *Profiles* the best it could be. Publicist Eileen Shapiro for her consistent direction and encouragement. John Pasquale for his friendship and support.

Producer/Editor Extraordinaire Monina Montenegro for being my right hand for over 20 years, your loyalty and friendship has been remarkable and treasured!

Lydia Loscalzo - Limos by Lydia for transporting our celebrities to and from our set for over two decades. Hair Stylist Doreen Pedreira for taking care of my hair for over twenty years. Snug Harbor Cultural Center for being our base of operations for over two decades. President and CEO Aileen Fuchs, Artie Colgan and Donald De Vincke for providing Security.

Special thanks to my close friends Jimmy Scara, Richie Murphy, Ed Tucker, Ronnie Farina and Bobby Knight. Missouri Valley College President Bonnie Humphrey and her right hand Eric Sappington for helping me return to my college roots. Monsignor Walter A. Birkle, Father Roy Cole and Father Bill Baker. My Mother Dorothy for making me the gentleman I aspire to be.

My Father Mickey Sr. for teaching me his street smarts and my Brother Mark. My daughter Katie who makes my life and all holidays special.

Lastly, to the over 500 celebrities who gave their time and energy to appear on *Profiles*... thank you for the memories!